William T. Blanford, George Albert Boulenger

On a Collection of Reptiles and Frogs Chiefly from Singapore

William T. Blanford, George Albert Boulenger

On a Collection of Reptiles and Frogs Chiefly from Singapore

ISBN/EAN: 9783337394844

Printed in Europe, USA, Canada, Australia, Japan

Cover: Foto ©Andreas Hilbeck / pixelio.de

More available books at **www.hansebooks.com**

.

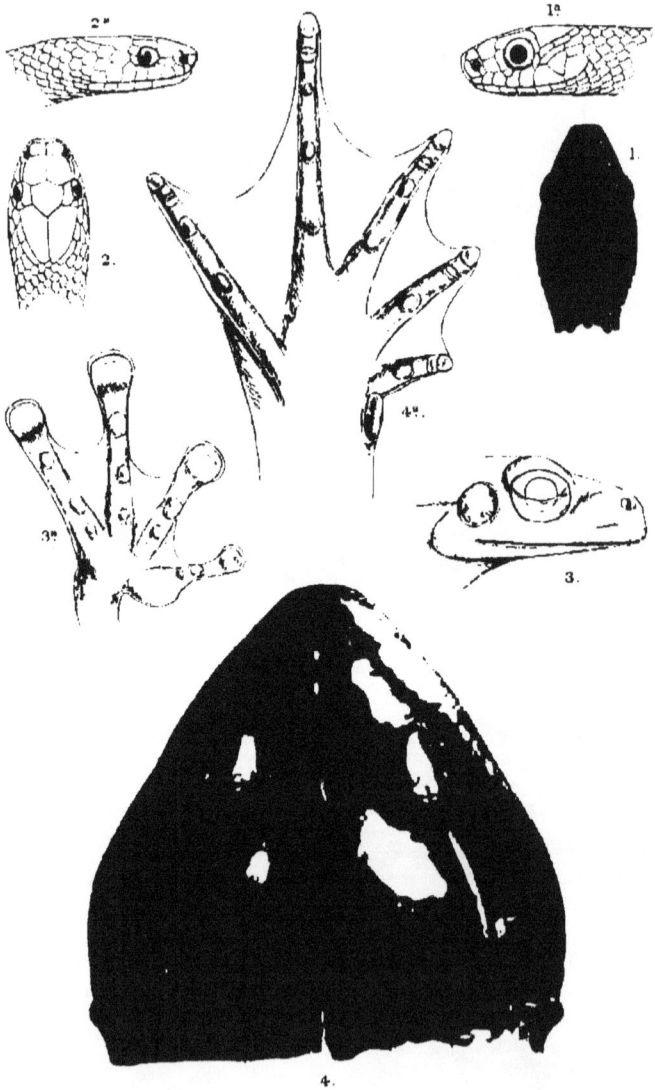

1 SIMOTES DENNYSI.   3.RHACOPHORUS DENNYSI.
2 OPHITES SUBCINCTUS. 4.RANA MACRODON.

3. On a Collection of Reptiles and Frogs chiefly from Singapore. By W. T. Blanford, F.R.S., F.Z.S., &c.

[Received September 21, 1880.]

(Plates XX. & XXI.)

Through the kindness of Dr. N. B. Dennys, I have had an opportunity of examining a collection of Reptiles and Frogs made at Singapore, and belonging to the Raffles Museum at that port. The
majority of the specimens were collected in the island of Singapore;
but a few are from other localities; and in the case of some of the
Lizards and Frogs, I am not quite certain whence they were originally obtained. Of all the Snakes (and these form the bulk of the
collection) the localities are appended. The number of new species
is small. It is evident that the Lizards and Frogs are but imperfectly represented; but the Snakes probably comprise, as I learn
from Dr. Dennys, nearly all the forms occurring at Singapore.

The following is a list of the species; those on which remarks are
added are distinguished by an asterisk (*). The nomenclature is
in most cases that employed by Dr. Günther in the ' Reptiles of
British India.'

REPTILIA.

LACERTILIA.

Hydrosaurus salvator.
*———, sp.
**Eumeces chinensis.*

Gecko guttatus.
Bronchocela cristatella.
Calotes versicolor.

OPHIDIA.

Typhlina lineata. Macassar.
Cylindrophis rufus. Singapore.
*——— *lineatus*, sp. nov. Sin-
gapore.
Xenopeltis unicolor. Singapore.
**Oxycalamus longiceps.* Singa-
pore.
Simotes octolineatus. Singa-
pore.
*——— *dennysi*, sp. nov. Singa-
pore.
Ablabes melanocephalus. Sin-
gapore.
**Nymphophidium subannulatum*
(Odontomus subannulatus,
D. & B.) Singapore.
Compsosoma melanurum. Sin-
gapore.
Dendrophis picta. Singapore.
——— caudolineata. Singapore.

**Ptyas mucosa.* Hongkong.
*——— *korros.* Singapore.
Tropidonotus quincunciatus.
Hongkong.
——— trianguligerus. Singapore.
——— stolatus. Singapore,
Hongkong.
——— rhodomelas. Macassar.
Cerberus rhynchops. Singa-
pore.
Homolopsis buccata. Singa-
pore.
Hipistes hydrinus. Singapore.
Chrysopelea ornata. Singapore,
Macassar.
Tragops prasinus. Singapore,
Macassar.
Dipsas cynodon. Singapore,
Sarawak.
——— dendrophila. Singapore.

Lycodon aulicus. Singapore, Macassar.
*Ophites subcinctus. Singapore.
Python reticulatus. Singapore.
*—— *curtus.* Singapore.
*Naja tripudians. Singapore.
Ophiophagus elaps. Singapore, Perak.
Bungarus fasciatus. Singapore.
—— *semifasciatus.* Honkong.
Callophis bivirgatus. Singapore.

Callophis intestinalis. Singapore, Macassar.
Platurus scutatus. Singapore.
*Hydrophis stokesi. Singapore.
*—— *viperina.* Macassar.
Pelamis bicolor. Singapore.
Trimeresurus gramineus. Singapore.
—— *erythrurus.* Singapore.
*—— *wagleri.* Singapore, Selangore.

AMPHIBIA.

BATRACHIA.

*Rana macrodon.
Megalophrys nasuta.

*Rhacophorus dennysi, sp. nov.
Bufo melanostictus.

HYDROSAURUS, sp.

Two young specimens of *Hydrosaurus,* of nearly the same size (13 and 14 inches long), occur in the collection. One of these is an undoubted example of the common *H. salvator*; the other differs somewhat both in the character of the head-scales and in coloration. The general proportions and the scales of the body, tail, and limbs appear similar in the two examples; there are about 80 transverse rows of ventral shields between the gular fold and the loin in the specimen agreeing with *H. salvator,* 77 in the other.

The differences in coloration, taken by themselves, would not be of much importance, there being some variation in most Monitors. The doubtful specimen is darker: the alternating rings of dark brown and white on the tail are more broken up into rows of spots; and narrow white rings occur in the intervals between the broader bands, whilst the white cross bands above the snout and the dark cross bands on the chin are wanting; they are, however, indicated on the sides of the head.

The more important distinctions are that the scales on the crown of the head in the abnormal specimen are smaller and marked by a central depression, and the enlarged superciliary scales are more numerous, 8 to 10 in number, instead of 5 or 6, and marked with a few comparatively large impressed dots instead of several minute spots. How far these characters are constant it is impossible to say without more specimens. It is probable that the two specimens are from different localities.

EUMECES CHINENSIS.

Tiliqua chinensis, Gray, Ann. Nat. Hist. ii. p. 289.
Mabouia chinensis, Günther, Rept. Brit. Ind. p. 83.

There is a single specimen, without locality, which must, I think, be referred to this species, though it presents several peculiarities.

The colour of the back is uniformly brown, there being no trace of the longitudinal pale bands usually found in this form; the præfrontal is wanting; the two postfrontals are slightly unequal and divided by a curved line; they are in contact with the supranasal: this is probably an individual peculiarity. There are also but 22 series of scales round the body instead of 24; about 34 occur in a longitudinal line between the axils of the fore and hind legs as in the type; and in other respects the specimen agrees with Chinese examples.

I am by no means sure that this form and its allies are really congeneric with *E. pavimentatus*, the type of the genus *Eumeces*. (See Peters, Monatsbericht Akad. Berl. 1864, p. 48; Stoliczka, J. A. S. B. 1870, xxxix. pt. 2, p. 174, and 1872, xli. pt. 2, p. 121; Anderson, P. A. S. B. 1871, xl. p. 181.) All these Scinks are very puzzling: and the generic distinctions accepted, such as the differences between smooth and keeled scales, transparent or scaly eyelid, presence or absence of supranasal shields, are scarcely of generic importance, and are merely convenient guides to identification.

CYLINDROPHIS LINEATUS, sp. nov.   (Plate XX.)

Head depressed, broad, short, the width between the eyes being equal to the length from the eye to the tip of the snout. Each frontal is as broad as long. The vertical is longer than broad, subtrapezoidal, the anterior margins meeting nearly at a right angle, the posterior termination slightly rounded. Supraorbitals longer than broad, each nearly equal in size to the vertical. Occipitals more than half as large as the vertical. Postocular very small, scarcely half the size of the first labial. Scales round the middle of the body in 21 rows. Ventrals, where widest, in the middle of the body, nearly twice the breadth of the scales on the sides; but the rows on each side of the ventrals are rather broader than the lateral and dorsal scales. Ventrals (from chin-shields to anal[1]) 215, two anals, subcaudals 9 besides the terminal scale.

Back longitudinally banded. A blackish-brown stripe, three scales wide, runs down the middle of the back from head to tail, and is bordered on each side by a narrower white band; below this again is a second, broad, blackish band of irregular width, with the lower border waved. This longitudinal band is separated by a narrow wavy white stripe from the transverse dark bands of the belly; the latter are wider than the alternating white bands; and, as in other species of the genus, the bands on the opposite sides of the abdomen do not precisely coincide. Head and tail yellowish white, with a few blackish spots.

Only a single specimen is sent. This measures 25 inches, of which the tail is 0·75 in. The Snake is probably rare.

Cylindrophis lineatus is distinguished from the three previously known species of the genus by its coloration, no other form exhi-

[1] It is difficult to say precisely where the true ventrals commence, as there is a gradual passage from the small scales immediately behind the chin-shields into the broader ventral shields.

biting longitudinal bands. It may be remarked that the distribu-
tion of colour appears to be very characteristic of the different forms
of *Cylindrophis*. But there are also structural peculiarities by
which the present form is separated from all previously described.

In the common species, *C. rufus*, all the head-shields are proportionally shorter, the frontals are broader than long, and the distance
between the eyes more than the length of the snout. The ventral
shields also are considerably less developed.

In *C. melanonotus* the vertical is still longer than in *C. lineatus*,
the sides of that shield behind the lateral angles converging much
less rapidly, and the occipitals are much smaller, each being barely
half the size of the vertical. The coloration, too, is quite different,
the back being uniformly dark brown.

In *C. maculatus*, the only other species known, the vertical, as in
C. melanonotus, is bell-shaped instead of subtrapezoidal, and the
occipitals are proportionally larger, being equal to the vertical in
size; the frontals are sometimes longer than the vertical. The
dorsal coloration consists of two rows of large pale spots, one on
each side of the median dorsal line, the intervening space being dark
brown.

The different species of the genus may be thus differentiated :—

A. The width between the eyes is more than the distance from the
   eye to the end of the snout.

1. *Cylindrophis rufus.* Back dark, with imperfect pale rings.
2. *C. melanonotus.* Back uniformly dark-coloured.

B. The width between the eyes is equal to the distance from the
   eye to the end of the snout.

3. *C. maculatus.* Back with large pale spots on a dark ground.
4. *C. lineatus.* Back longitudinally banded.

OXYCALAMUS LONGICEPS.

Calamaria longiceps, Cantor, J. A. S. B. 1847, xvi. p. 910, pl. xl.
fig. 1.
Oxycalamus longiceps, Günther, Rept. Brit. India, p. 199 ; Stoliczka, J. A. S. B. 1873, xlii. pt. 2, p. 120.

Two specimens of this Snake are sent ; they measure 6½ and
7 inches respectively. The nasal shield is single, as noted by Cantor
and Stoliczka ; but it is divided by a suture below the nostril. Ventrals 143 in one, 128 in the other, subcaudals 19 and 25 pairs.

Both specimens have an imperfect pale collar a little behind the
head ; and one has a light spot on the hinder part of the fifth labial,
extending to the occipital shield. Similar coloration is noted by
Stoliczka in a Penang specimen.

SIMOTES DENNYSI, sp. nov.   (Plate XXI. fig. 1.)

Scales in 21 rows. General form stout and short, as in *S. cochinchinensis* [1] and *S. catenifer* [2] ; the head broader than the neck.

[1] Günther, Rept. Brit. Ind. p. 219, pl. xx. fig. C.
[2] Stoliczka, J. A. S. B. 1873, xlii. pt. 2. p. 121, pl. xi. fig. 3.

Rostral well developed ; præfrontals more than half as large as postfrontals, the suture between the former but little shorter than that between the latter. Vertical large, pentagonal, the anterior margin convex, lateral edges converging slightly behind, posterior margins meeting at a right angle. Each occipital is both longer and broader than the vertical, and is rounded behind.

Loreal well developed, about as high as broad. Two (or three) præoculars, the upper double the size of the lower ; two postoculars ; temporals 2 + 3, the upper anterior temporal shield in contact with both postoculars ; two elongate temporals along the outer side of each occipital. Upper labials 8, the seventh excluded from the margin of the lip, the fourth and fifth (or on one side the fifth only) entering the orbit. Two pairs of chin-shields, the posterior but little shorter than the anterior.

Ventral shields 175 ; anal undivided ; subcaudals in 50 pairs, with a long terminal scale.

Back grey, with eleven dark-brown cross bands or large transverse spots on the body, and four on the tail, all having very irregular zigzag margins, and being, where widest, about half the breadth of the interspaces ; the latter are slightly spotted and mottled with brown. On the head there is a broad dark cross band between the anterior parts of the eye-orbits on the front part of the vertical and on both pairs of frontals, and continued below the eye on the fifth and sixth supralabials. Behind this is a pointed elongated arrowhead-shaped dark mark, joining the anterior band on the vertical shield, and bifurcating behind on the neck ; there is also an oblique band just behind the angle of the mouth. Belly whitish, with small quadrangular dark spots on the sides of every second or third ventral.

A single specimen is sent ; it is only 8 inches long, the tail measuring 1¼.

This is another species of the peculiar group of *Simotes* comprising S. cochinchinensis, S. brevicauda [1], S. catenifer, and S. ancoralis [2]. It is distinguished from all by having the seventh supralabial shield shut out of the lip-margin, and from all but the first by having twenty-one rows of scales. The coloration, too, differs somewhat from that of S. cochinchinensis, in which the lower parts are white.

NYMPHOPHIDIUM SUBANNULATUM.

Odontomus subannulatus, Dum. et Bibr. Erp. Gén. vii. p. 454 ; Jan & Sordelli, Icon. Oph. 36ᵉ livr. pl. v. fig. 3.

I had already identified the single specimen in the collection with the snake described by Duméril and Bibron, and figured by Jan [3],

---

[1] Steindachner, Novara Rept. p. 61, pl. iii. figs. 13–14.

[2] Jan, Icon. Gen. Oph. 11ᵉ livr. pl. 6. fig. 2 : see Stoliczka, J. A. S. B. 1873, xlii. p. 122.

[3] The specimen described by the first-named writers, the only one they had seen, was from the Leyden Museum ; and as Jan's figure was taken from a snake belonging to the same collection, it is probable that the same individual was examined by both authors. The dimensions agree.

when Dr. Günther called my attention to the dentition, and suggested that the species might be a *Nymphophidium*. On comparing it with the type of *N. maculatum* in the British Museum, I found a close agreement in all essential characters; but some differences in the form of the head-shields and in the dentition show, I think, that the species are distinct.

The pupil in the snake now described is distinctly vertical; and this character is shown in Jan's figure of *Odontomus subannulatus*, although it is not mentioned in Duméril and Bibron's rather meagre description. From Günther's description of *Nymphophidium*, it might be inferred that the pupil is round, as it is in *Odontomus* as restricted by Günther; for the two genera are said to agree in every respect except dentition. On examining the type of *N. maculatum* in the British Museum, however, I find that the pupils are ill-preserved, and their form is not distinguishable; but in a second specimen, procured from Dr. Bleeker for the same collection, the pupil on one side is slightly elliptical. This very peculiar feature of a vertical pupil has consequently to be added to the generic characters. I find in the present specimen of *N. subannulatum* two peculiar small conical white tooth-like projections from the base of the skull, as in *N. maculatum*. They are easily seen at the back of the palate when the mouth is opened freely.

I add a description of the present snake, Duméril and Bibron's account being (as already noticed) imperfect.

Description.—Body and tail slender, compressed. Head much broader than neck, flat, depressed. Pupil elliptical, vertical. Scales of body but little longer than broad, smooth, in 15 rows. Ventrals 230, strongly angulate at the sides; anal undivided; subcaudals in 97 pairs. Maxillary teeth small and numerous, increasing slightly in size behind; the last is much larger and compressed, and projects horizontally backwards.

Head-shields.—Rostral broader than high, scarcely extending to the upper surface of the head. Anterior frontals as long as the posterior, rounded in front, scarcely broader than long. Posterior frontals much broader than long. Vertical elongate, the lateral margins converging and slightly concave, posterior angle acute; the length of the shield is but little less than that of an occipital; and the postfrontals and vertical together considerably exceed the occipitals in length. Nostril near the middle of a single rectangular shield, succeeded behind by another elongate rectangular shield (the loreal, or loreal and lower præocular united), which extends to the eye. A small præocular above the loreal, one postocular [1]. Temporals 2+2. Supralabials 7, the third and fourth enter the orbit.

Colour (in spirit). The anterior portion of the back dark brown, with subdistant pale cross bands, which become closer together

---

[1] In this character the specimen appears to differ from the type, which is figured with two postoculars. But on one side of the present example there is a well-marked groove, if not an imperfect suture, separating the lower posterior portion of the superciliary shield; and the postocular precisely corresponds to the inferior postorbital of the figure.

behind, and then intersect the dark areas, until on the posterior part of the back and tail there is a double row of brown spots. The white bands expand at the side, and, except near the head, bifurcate around a dark spot. Lower parts whitish. Head with a rather broad central dark band throughout the vertical and occipitals, and joined behind to the large brown spot on the back of the neck; the sides of the vertical and occipitals, with the greater part of the sides of the head and neck, are pale; but there is a dark patch on each superciliary shield, another on the temporals on each side, and the greater part of the snout in front of the eyes is dark brown.

Length of the specimen 13 inches, of which the tail is 3·1, or nearly one fourth.

The principal characters by which this form may be distinguished from *N. maculatum* are:—(1) The greater length of the vertical shield: in *N. maculatum* the vertical is much shorter than an occipital, the latter being equal in length to the vertical and post-frontals together; in *N. subannulatum* the vertical and postfrontals together are much longer than an occipital. (2) Dentition, there being only one larger tooth at the back of the jaw. In *N. maculatum* the nasals are described as separated by an indistinct suture; but I cannot detect with certainty a suture in the type; and in the second specimen the nasal is certainly undivided [1].

I think it not impossible that the genus *Ulupe*, described by me [2] in 1878 from a Tenasserim specimen, is allied to *Nymphophidium*. *Ulupe* has but 13 rows of scales round the body, and there is no præocular above the elongate loreal: but in other respects the genus approaches *Nymphophidium* very closely. I am far from certain that I was right in assigning *Ulupe* to the *Lycodontidæ*, to which, it should be remembered, *Odontomus* was referred by Duméril and Bibron, although Günther afterwards showed that the dentition differed from the Lycodont type.

PTYAS MUCOSA and PT. KORROS.

There are five specimens belonging to the genus *Ptyas*. One has 15 scales round the middle of the body, two have 16, and two 17; in the latter there are 3 loreals; all have the dorsal scales distinctly keeled on the posterior portion of the body. I refer the first three to *Pt. korros*, the latter two to *Pt. mucosa*; but I believe all to belong to one specific form and not to deserve to be distinguished, except as varieties. Since determining the specimens, I have ascertained that the individuals referred to *Pt. mucosa* are from Hong-Kong.

TROPIDONOTUS RHODOMELAS.

Tropidonotus rhodomelas, Boie, Isis, 1827, p. 535; Schlegel, Phys. Serp. i. p. 167, ii. p. 310, pl. xii. f. 10, 11.

[1] In Jan's figure of *Odontomus subannulatus* a suture is shown below the nostril, but not above. In the specimen examined by me there is on one side a slight groove below the nostril, but no suture.
[2] J. A. S. B. 1878. vol. xlvii. pt. 2, p. 128.

Amphiesma rhodomelas, Duméril & Bibron, Erp. Gén. vii. p. 737.

Xenodon rhodomelas, Günther, Cat. Snakes B. M. 1858, p. 58.

Three specimens from Macassar, one quite small, only 8 inches long, the other two 22 and 23½ inches in length. In all there are two præoculars, the lower being very small; one (the young) specimen has three, the other two have each four postoculars[1]. In one example there are eight supralabials on one side, the second being divided. The loreal is about as high as broad, but only the hinder part of the upper margin slopes downwards, and the form of the shield appears rather variable.

Ventrals 131, 133, and 134; anal divided; subcaudals 52 pairs in two specimens, 55 in the third. These numbers are a little higher than those given by Duméril and Bibron.

OPHITES SUBCINCTUS, var. (Plate XXI. fig. 2.)

Besides two normal specimens of this species, there is in the collection a young snake, 10¾ inches long (of which the tail measures 2), with smooth scales, and an undivided anal, but otherwise agreeing with *O. subcinctus,* and having the same peculiar arrangement of shields in the loreal region. In consequence of the scales being smooth, I at first took this for an undescribed species of the genus *Tnycodon,* and had the accompanying figures of the head prepared, but subsequently amongst some snakes from province Wellesley in Malacca, collected by Mr. W. L. Distant, I found a much larger specimen of *Ophites subcinctus,* in which the keels of the dorsal scales were very faint in the hinder part of the body, and quite absent in the anterior portion. I therefore now consider the young Singapore snake an abnormal specimen of the same species.

PYTHON CURTUS.

Python curtus, Schlegel, apud Hubrecht, Notes from the Museum at Leyden, vol. i. p. 244[2].

This is a very remarkable species of *Python*: and it is curious that it should so long have escaped notice, Hubrecht's description having only been published last year. The specimen in the Leyden Museum was from Sumatra.

P. curtus is remarkably stout for its length, its girth being proportionally much greater than that of *P. reticulatus* and *P. molurus.* The number of scales round the body is less, the ventrals and sub-

[1] Duméril and Bibron say one præ- and two postoculars. Schlegel represents one præ- and four postoculars; but the figure does not look very exact in this respect.

[2] In the 'Zoological Record' for 1877 there is the following notice:— "*Python curtus,* Schleg. Description and figure; A. Hubrecht, Ann. Mus. Leyd. No. 1." I learn that the work quoted has not been published; but a titlepage and, I believe, the figure and description of the present species were printed and a copy sent to the Recorder. In the 'Notes from the Museum at Leyden,' published in 1879, it is stated that the 'Annals,' which will contain a full description and figure of this species, will be published shortly.

caudals are considerably less numerous, and the tail is much shorter. The coloration, too, is different.

The following is a description of the specimen from Singapore:— Three pairs of frontals; vertical divided; enlarged irregularly shaped plates covering the occipital region. Nostril on the upper surface of the head, between two plates, the hinder of which is very small; a row of small scales extends from the nostril to the eye. Rostral and the two anterior upper labials on each side with deep elongate pits; ten upper labials; the fifth and sixth enter the orbit. Three or four of the anterior lower labials pitted; a longitudinal groove along most of the posterior lower labial shields.

Scales in 55 rows round the middle of the body, the series on each side of the ventrals being nearly half as broad as the latter. Ventrals 175; anal entire; subcaudals 32 pairs.

Colour (in spirit). The upper part of the head is uniformly earthy-grey, almost ash-grey, with a narrow pale median streak running back for some distance from the occiput; upper labials the same; a dark brown mark in front of the eye, continued behind the eye and expanding into a broad brown band, dark at the edges, and especially along the upper margin; this band runs down the side of the neck, and is succeeded by a row of large brown dark-edged spots along the anterior portion of the body. Back fawn-colour, with a row of rather irregular pale spots along the middle; below the fawn-coloured band and above the dark spots is a light belt with small dark brown spots on many of the scales. The coloration of the dorsal parts continues to the tail, which is dark brown above, light brown below, pale on the sides. Lower parts, except of the tail, white.

In the number of scales round the body, and of the ventrals and subcaudals, this form closely resembles the West-African *P. regius*; but that species, like the other African Pythons, has the nostrils laterally placed and the four anterior upper labials pitted, besides other differences.

The single specimen received, which is in magnificent condition, measures 55 inches in length, of which the tail is only 4; the girth round the middle of the body is 8·5 inches. A specimen of *P. reticulatus*, 67 inches long, has the tail 8·5 inches in length, and a girth of only 5·5 inches.

Dr. Dennys writes to me that he has seen but two specimens of this *Python*, one of which escaped from its cage and was lost.

NAJA TRIPUDIANS.

Both the specimens in the collection are black throughout, without any marks on the back of the hood, but with some pale spots on the side of the neck and beneath it.

HYDROPHIS STOKESI.

Günther (Rept. Brit. Ind. p. 363) speaks of the occurrence of this species in the Chinese seas and the East Indian archipelago as doubtful. I think, however, that two specimens sent must be referred to this form, although they differ somewhat from the Australian types. One is a fine example, 64 inches long; the other is young, and measures but 16½ inches. Both have only 39 scales round the neck, instead of from 43 to 47; but I can find no other structural distinction, and a larger series would be necessary in order to show whether this difference is constant. The larger specimen has alternating black and yellow rings quite round the body; the younger has the black rings not quite perfect.

HYDROPHIS VIPERINA.

Hydrophis viperina, Günther, Rept. Brit. Ind. p. 378; Anderson, P. Z. S. 1872, p. 400.

The single specimen sent is 26 inches long. The colour differs but little from that of the much smaller type in the British Museum.

TRIMERESURUS WAGLERI.

There are two specimens of this Snake, 23 and 32½ inches in length. Both have 25 scales round the middle of the body. The prevailing colour in both is gamboge-yellow; the smaller has narrow yellow rings alternating with much broader bands composed of pale greenish scales with black margins; in the larger specimen the transverse bands are very indistinct, black scales, yellow scales, and black-edged scales being intermingled.

There is also a smaller *Trimeresurus*, 17½ inches long, with but 21 rows of scales round the middle of the body, grass-green above, with very minute subdistant spots, white in front, brown behind, about 5 or 6 scales apart from each other, arranged in a line down each side of the back. This agrees with *T. maculatus*, Gray, said by Günther, Rept. Brit. India, p. 388, to be the young of *T. wagleri*.

I find, however, in the British-Museum collection, specimens, chiefly from Borneo, that appear to show a gradation between these widely different forms. Two of the smaller specimens from Borneo, with the coloration of *T. maculatus*, have, the one 21, the other 22 scales round the middle of the body. It is evident the number in this species varies from 21 to 25, if *T. maculatus* is really the same as *T. wagleri*. In all adult or nearly adult specimens of the latter I find 25 rows of scales.

RHACOPHORUS DENNYSI, sp. nov. (Plate XXI. fig. 3.)

Size of *R. maximus*. Colour above, in spirits, dark violet, almost slaty, below dirty white mottled with dusky, a brown spot behind the occiput. The tympanum is very little smaller than the eye. The nostril opens backward. The web between the toes without dark spots and deeply emarginate; it extends to the pads at the end of all the toes of the hind feet; but it is very narrow near the end of the fourth toe on each side. *The fingers are incompletely webbed*, the web not extending to the end of any digit; the terminal phalanx of the third or longest digit is quite free. The projection on the inside of the inner finger is flat as in *R. reinwardti*, and has not a tubercle beneath it as in *R. maximus*. Folds along the edges of

PLATE XXVI.

1.

2.

Mintern Bros. imp.

G. Mintern del.

the limbs inconspicuous. The length of the manus from the wrist to the tip of the longest finger is nearly equal to the width of the head. Vomerine teeth in two straight ridges, nearly in the same right line ; the distance of the two series apart is scarcely more than half the length of each series ; the ridges commence from the anterior inner margins of the inner nostrils.

		inches.
Length of head and body		4·5
„	hind limb from anus to end of longest toe	6·75
„	foot	2
„	hand	1·45

This species much resembles the East-Himalayan and Assamese *R. maximus*, which it equals or excels in size ; but the tympanum is proportionally twice as large, and the webs of the feet are less developed (they are shorter in the fore feet of *R. maximus* than in those of *R. reinwardti* or *R. malabaricus*). From *R. reinwardti* the new form is distinguished by size, coloration, and by the fingers being imperfectly webbed.

The single specimen sent, Dr. Dennys informs me, was of a beautiful emerald-green colour when alive, and belonged to a well-known Chinese merchant named Whampoa, who refused an offer of five hundred dollars for it. When the animal died, it was presented to the Raffles Museum. It is said to have originally come from China ; but the precise locality is not known.

In the smaller forms of *Rhacophorus*, the development of the folds of skin along the sides of the limbs and above the anus is very remarkable. Mr. Wood-Mason called my attention to this in the case of *R. maculatus* (and I find the same in *R. reinwardti*), and noticed that this form shows a passage towards the curious Flying Frog of Borneo figured by Wallace in the ‘ Malay Archipelago,’ vol. i. p. 60.

RANA MACRODON. (Plate XXI. fig. 4.)

I am indebted to M. Boulenger for the identification of this species. The specimens differ considerably from the descriptions given by Duméril and Bibron[1], and by Günther[2], both of whom describe the tympanum as small. This character, however, is, I learn from M. Boulenger, more variable than has hitherto been supposed ; and as there is, in the British Museum, a specimen from Java, the original locality of the species, that agrees with those from Singapore, I accept M. Boulenger's opinion. The following is a description of the Singapore specimens.

Head very broad and flat—the breadth across the gape being greater than the distance from gape to muzzle, and equal to the length of the hind foot in females, exceeding it by one eighth to one tenth in males. Snout depressed, rounded at the end ; no trace of *canthus rostralis* ; the nostrils near the end of the snout and distant from the eye, their distance apart being about half of the in-

[1] Erp. Gén. viii. p. 382.   [2] Brit.-Mus. Cat. Batr. Sal. p. 8.

terval between nostril and eye. Eye of moderate size, the diameter
about equal to the length of the fourth finger. Tympanum distinct,
nearly as large as the eye. Lower jaw with two prominent apophyses
in front, fitting into hollows inside the upper jaw; in a female sent
these apophyses are inconspicuous. Vomerine teeth on two straight
ridges running obliquely back from the interior angle of the inner
nostrils, and converging behind so as to meet, if prolonged, nearly in
a right angle, but rather widely separated; a strong osseous transverse
ridge behind the choanæ. No vocal sac. A strong fold from behind
the eye running horizontally to over the tympanum, then turned down
at an obtuse angle and running to the shoulder. Posterior portion
of upper eyelid tubercular. Skin of body and limbs smooth. Limbs
stout, the tips of both toes and fingers slightly swollen; the distance
from vent to knee is about half the length of the body from snout
to vent or a little more; from vent to metatarsal tubercle is longer than
the body. The metatarsal tubercle is elongate, not flattened. The
toes are scarcely fully webbed; the terminal two phalanges of the
fourth toe have only a narrow fringe along their sides, and the web
is deeply emarginate; a narrow fold along the inside of the foot.

Colour (in spirits) light brown above, one specimen (a male) having
a pale stripe down the back, very little paler below, the sides and
lower portion of the limbs, the sides of the body, breast and chin
marbled with rich brown.

	♂ inches.	♀ inches.
Length from nose to vent	6	4·9
„ of head	2·6	1·7
Breadth of head	3·15	2·2
Length of hind leg	8·6	7·5
„ hind foot	2·65	2·15

Three specimens are sent—two apparently males, the third a
female. I believe all were obtained at Singapore; but I have not
heard positively that this was the case.

This form is closely allied to *Rana fusca*[1], but has a much
broader head; the eye is smaller, and the tympanum larger; the
muzzle is flatter, the nostrils nearer together, and the web between
the toes of the hind feet much less developed.

In the specimens of *R. fusca* from Penang, described by Stoliczka,
there does not appear to be any passage towards the Singapore form;
for the toes are said to be fully webbed. Mr. Boulenger informs
me that he considers *R. fusca* also a variety of *R. macrodon*.

In the Journal of the Asiatic Society of Bengal for 1879, vol.
xlviii. pt. 2, p. 130, I described a supposed new species of *Hypsirhina* under the name of *H. maculata*. I overlooked the fact that
this name had previously been given by Duméril and Bibron to the
Chinese species *H. bennetti*. Under these circumstances I propose
to change the name of the Burmese form to *Hypsirhina maculosa*.

[1] Blyth, J. A. S. B. xxiv. 1855, p. 719 (the volume is wrongly quoted by Anderson as xxxiv); Theobald, "Cat. Rept.," J. A. S. B. 1868, extra number, p. 79;
Anderson, P. Z. S. 1871, p. 197; Stoliczka, J. A. S. B. 1873, xlii. pt. 2, p. 115.

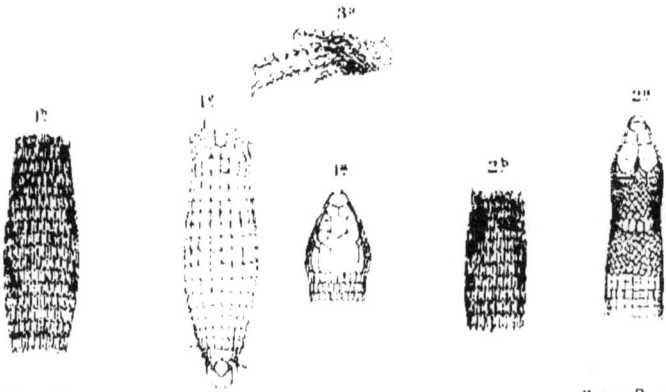

1. CERCOSAURA RETICULATA.
2. LEPOSOMA BUCKLEYI.
3. CERCOSAURA MANICATA.

J. Mintern lith.

Mintern. Bros. imp.

1. ECPLEOPUS (EUSPONDYLUS) GUENTHERI.
2. GONIODACTYLUS CONCINNATUS.
3. BUCKLEYI.

EXPLANATION OF THE PLATES.

PLATE XX.

Cylindrophis lineatus, sp. nov., p. 217; with outlines of head-shields, from above.

PLATE XXI.

Fig. 1. *Simotes dennysi*, sp. nov., view of head, p. 218; from above.
   1*a*. —— ——, outline of head-shields, side view.
   2. *Ophites subcinctus*, var., p. 222; outline of head-shields, from above.
   2*a*. —— ——, var., outline of head-shields, side view.
   3. *Rhacophorus dennysi*, sp. nov., p. 224; side of head.
   3*a*. —— ——, fore foot, from below.
   4. *Rana macrodon*, p. 225; head.
   4*a*. —— ——, hind foot, from below.

All the above figures are of the natural size, except 1, 1*a*, 2, and 2*a*, which are
double the real dimensions.

---

4. An Account of the Collection of Lizards made by Mr.
Buckley in Ecuador, and now in the British Museum,
with Descriptions of the new Species. By the late A.
W. E. O'SHAUGHNESSY, Esq., Assistant in the Natural-
History Departments, British Museum.

[Received January 19, 1881.]

(Plates XXII.–XXV.)

Of the zoological collections made by Mr. Buckley in Ecuador,
various sections of which have already formed the subjects of papers
in these ' Proceedings,' not the least interesting is the collection of
Lizards, both on account of the number of new species it reveals, and
because of the fresh materials it affords for the study of those already
known. I have given a partial notice of this collection (P. Z. S.
1880, p. 491), confined, however, to a preliminary list of the species
of *Anolis* identified, and the description of a beautiful new one. I
now offer the results of a study of the whole collection, and have
thought it advisable not to restrict the present paper to the description of the new forms, but to enumerate all the species, for the purpose of recording additional remarks and revisions which have
appeared necessary, and of thus making this contribution to the
Herpetology of Ecuador as complete as possible. A much earlier
collection, that of Mr. Fraser, afforded Dr. Günther the opportunity,
in 1859, of describing and figuring a series of reptiles from the same
region (P. Z. S. 1859, p. 89); and his paper has, of course, been
frequently referred to.

I may point out that the family Cercosauridæ, our knowledge of
which, so imperfect before Prof. Peters's admirable memoir in 1863,
had scarcely been increased since that date, has received some
remarkable accessions in the present collection; also that the genus
Enyalius has been further worked out, whilst a new form of the
curious genus *Hoplocercus* has been brought to light.

15*

The specimens were collected at three distinct stations:—viz.
Canelos, Pallatanga, and Sarayacu.

TEJIDÆ.

1. CENTROPYX DORSALIS, Günther.

Monoplocus dorsalis, Günther, P. Z. S. 1859, p. 404.
Centropyx pelviceps, Cope, Pr. Ac. Phil. 1868, p. 98.
? *Centropyx altamazonicus*, Cope, J. Ac. Phil. (n. s.) viii. 1876,
p. 162.

Two specimens, the largest measuring about 11½ inches long,
from Canelos. Another good-sized specimen, from the Peruvian
Amazons, is also in the British Museum. By its keeled præanal
scutes this species would be the *C. altamazonicus*, Cope, rather than
his *C. pelviceps*; but I am inclined to think that the very small
specimen on which the former is founded will prove identical with
the latter. If so, both must be referred to the species described by
Dr. Günther, also on a small type specimen, in which, after renewed examination, I do not find that the distinctions relied on by
Prof. Cope when describing *C. pelviceps* hold good, as I count
fourteen longitudinal series of ventrals in the middle of the body,
and can also distinguish femoral pores. The largest specimen from
Canelos has the sixteen ventral series characteristic of *C. altamazonicus*, though that species shows them already in a young specimen. I may add that Dr. Günther's type possesses the anal spurs
of this genus.

2. NEUSTICURUS ECPLEOPUS.

Neusticurus ecpleopus, Cope, J. Ac. Phil. 1876, p. 161; O'Shaugh.
Ann. N. H. ser. 5, vol. iv. p. 295 (1879).

Pallatanga.

CERCOSAURIDÆ.

Emminia olivacea of Gray is a *Cercosaura*, as was rightly surmised
by Dr. Peters in 1863; moreover it is so closely related to *Cercosaura ocellata*, Wagler, that nothing but the conspicuous lateral
ocelli and the three additional femoral pores of that species separate
them. With regard to the præanal scutes, I may mention that
another specimen from Para, which, some time since, I had occasion
to add to the named series in the British Museum, has the two large
plates figured by Peters as belonging to Wagler's species, instead of
the four smaller marginal plates of Gray's type; but on this ground
alone I should not venture to separate it from *C. olivacea*, with
which it agrees exactly in every detail. It is perhaps superfluous
to state that no foundation for the peculiar position assigned to the
nostril by Dr. Gray is afforded by the specimen.

A similar variability in the arrangement of the præanal scutes,
associated with an irregularity in the plates of the muzzle, is shown
in a series of four specimens, which, however, cannot be specifically
distinct, and are doubtless referrable to the species described by Prof.

Peters as *Cercosaura (Pantodactylus) argulus.* Although the
number and arrangement of the præanal scutes affords a conspicuous and important character in the family Cercosauridæ, and in many
cases a reliable one, sufficing, for instance, to distinguish several
species of *Leposoma* from the original one of Spix, and from the new
one recently described by Prof. Peters, allowance must be made for
a certain amount of variation in this particular, more especially as
corresponding variations in other characteristic portions of the scutellation are to be found in the Lizards of this and closely allied
South-American groups.

I have already noticed that the internasal plate is sometimes
entire and sometimes bisected in *Neusticurus ecpleopus,* Cope, although
this species was described by Prof. Cope as differing from *N. bicarinatus,* L., in having it entire (see 'Ann. N. H.' Oct. 1879, p. 295).
I found also in *N. bicarinatus* an irregular additional præfrontal
plate associated with the cleft internasal. In the present series of
specimens of *Cercosaura (Pantodactylus) argulus,* the internasal
has a longitudinal cleft in a line with the suture of the fronto-nasals,
and occasionally the above-mentioned supernumerary plate is present in exactly the same position as in *Neusticus bicarinatus.* The
fronto-nasals are in that case reduced to smaller triangular and more
lateral plates, quite separated from each other, instead of being large
and extensively in contact. These two forms of arrangement of the
nasal shields are associated with two distinct types of præanal scutellation. One specimen with the additional præfrontal has four
narrow marginal præanals; another with the normal nasal plates
has only two large rounded marginal præanals, like *Cercosaura ocellata,* while the others have the normal nasals and the four narrow
marginal præanals.

As Prof. Peters had only a single specimen from Bogota,
and those in the present collection from Ecuador show a range of
variation within recognizable specific limits, I give the following
supplementary description :—

3. CERCOSAURA (PANTODACTYLUS) ARGULUS, Peters, Abh. Ak.
Berl. 1863, p. 184, pl. i. fig. 3.

Internasal broad, single, or bisected in a line with the suture of
the two good-sized fronto-nasals when these are extensively in contact; sometimes an intermediate small præfrontal joining the frontal
and the internasal. Frontal and fronto-parietals of the ordinary
shape, interparietal large, flanked by two large parietals, and followed by a small occipital enclosed between two good-sized postoc-
cipital plates. Nasal rather large, followed by a single large frenal.
Supralabials six, none particularly elongate; infralabials five, the third
very elongate. Two pairs of large postmentals in contact, the third
smaller, separated by the group of large and small intervening gular
scales. Two contiguous rows of larger plates to the chest, where a
small collar is formed by a central and two lateral rounded plates.
Some convex scales behind the occiput; scales of the back not very
narrow, keeled, pointed, the keels being slightly produced; on the

sides small quadrate scales, in two rows to each of the dorsal rows. Ventral plates large, in six longitudinal series, the middle ones squarish, the outer rounded. Præanal scutes four or six, arranged as described above. Four series of square, smooth, inferior caudal plates; those above elongated, keeled, without points. Tail generally with a lateral groove. Femoral pores six to nine.

Above light brown; head variegated with darker. A central dark longitudinal stripe and a lateral one on each side, beneath which a light vitta extends from the temporal region the whole length of the side, again bordered inferiorly with black. Sides with a series of eight or nine large ocelli black with white centres; another, pure white, lower lateral stripe from the labials and beneath the eye. Entire ventral surface yellowish; each ventral, anal, and lower caudal scute with a central black dot. Tail above and below light brown or yellowish, the dorsal tints fading and the stripes ceasing over the rump.

		millim.
Total length		102
Distance of tip of snout from ear-opening..		12
,, ,, ,, fore limb ..		18
,, ,, ,, vent		43
Length of fore limb		15
,, fourth finger on fore limb......		4
,, hind limb		20
,, third hind toe		4½
,, fourth hind toe		5½

Beside the other differences noted above, Prof. Peters's type specimen showed only two anterior lateral ocelli. Its locality is given as the mountain region of Santa Fé de Bogota. Of the four collected by Mr. Buckley in Ecuador, one is from Pallatanga, and three are from Canelos.

4. CERCOSAURA (PANTODACTYLUS) RETICULATA, sp. n. (Plate XXII. fig. 1).

Internasal broad, fronto-nasals pentagonal, with one side in contact; frontal short; fronto-parietals separate; interparietal long and straight; parietals also with straight inner edge, broader than the interparietal, and rounded externally; these three plates evenly truncate on the posterior line of the head, and followed by two transverse rows of small plates, preceding the regular scales of the nape, there being no true occipital shields. Head-shields smooth, without any ridges. Supraorbitals three. One frenal. Supralabials seven, none of them elongate; infralabials six. Temporal scales irregular, polygonal, rather large. A single mental shield behind the symphysial, and four pairs of postmentals, the two first in contact, the others separated by narrow intervening scales. A double series of large gular shields ending in the very indistinct collar before the chest. Scales of the entire upper surface and sides of the body very narrow, elongate, and keeled, of the same type as those of *C. schreibersii*, but narrower. Sides of the neck and shoulder granular. Ventral shields smooth, in eight longitudinal series, long, narrow, and distinctly rounded posteriorly. Four principal præanal shields—two median, with their points touching, and two lateral. Tail continuing the scutellation of the back and ventral surface, with a distinct groove along the side. Second and fifth toes on fore foot nearly equal ; fourth a little longer than the third.

Brown, variegated with black on the head, with close longitudinal series of light black-edged ocelli or of light spots, in a black longitudinal stripe on the back and sides of the body. Labials and chinshields spotted with black. Tail pale yellowish brown. Entire undersurface yellowish.

	millim.
Total length	114
Distance from tip of snout to ear-opening	10
„ „ „ fore limb	18
„ „ „ vent	43
Length of fore limb	11
„ fourth front toe	3
„ hind limb	18
„ third hind toe	4
„ fourth hind toe	6

This species has the dorsal scutellation characteristic of the subgenus *Pantodactylus* ; but, as before remarked, the dorsal scales are still narrower than in *Cercosaura schreibersii*, and more like those of *C. argulus*, Peters, figured in 'Abh. Ak. Berl.' 1863, pl. i. fig. 3. The narrow rounded ventral scales are a peculiar feature ; and so also is the arrangement of the parietal head-shields, which is like that of the genus *Leposoma*.

One specimen from Canelos.

CERCOSAURA, subg. n. PRIONODACTYLUS.

Characters of *Cercosaura* and of the section *Pantodactylus*. Toes of both fore and hind feet strongly toothed beneath.

5. CERCOSAURA (PRIONODACTYLUS) MANICATA, subg. et sp. nn. (Plate XXII. fig. 3.)

A single broad internasal, two fronto-nasals in contact, the rest of the plates on the upper surface of the head as in *C. schreibersii*, the interparietal being somewhat shorter. A single frenal, a large triangular præocular over the labials, and another similar canthal plate before the supraorbitals. Six supralabials, the third, fourth, and sixth elongate, continued in a series of longish smooth plates in the same line as far as the ear-opening ; only four infralabials, the third extremely elongate. A single broad mental plate behind the symphysial, followed by two pairs of contiguous posterior plates, a third pair being widely separated and forced into a lateral position by two converging groups of large oval gular scales, the central and lateral gular spaces being occupied by smaller rounded scales ; a double row of very large broad plates, increasing in size posteriorly, leading to the chest.

Sides of the neck and of the body anteriorly granular. Back covered entirely with elongate narrow, strongly keeled scales, sharply pointed posteriorly, in about eighteen longitudinal rows in the middle of the body, and giving place to much smaller scales on the sides. Ventral shields large and smooth, the middle ones square, the lateral ones rounded, in six longitudinal series, with an additional small external series on each side. Three posterior very long præanal shields, the middle one very narrow and straight, the two outer ones broader and rounded. Lower caudal plates smooth, the upper ones, continued from the back, keeled. Limbs with large scutes on the anterior surfaces, as in other Lizards of this group.

Fourth toe on the anterior limb a little longer than the third. The scales beneath the toes with tooth-like projections; so that all the toes on both fore and hind feet are strongly pectinate.

Femoral pores twelve.

Dark greenish above (in spirits). The sides black, forming a broad and well-defined stripe from the sides of the head to the tail, bounded inferiorly by a narrow pure white stripe from the rostral to the hind limb. A very remarkable pure white patch covers a part of the fore limb, including the first, second, and third toes, and reaching up the wrist and along the anterior scutes of the inner surface of the arms to the elbow. Another isolated white patch is seen on the fore part of the upper arm, near the body. The rest of the front or upper surfaces of the fore limb are dark brown, black in the vicinity of the white patches, and including the two remaining toes. The hind limbs are paler brown, with faint coloured ocelli. Lower surface of the entire Lizard yellowish white, becoming bluish on the belly. The upper surface of the trunk is variegated with dark spots and a distinct zigzag pattern of light and dark brown extends the whole length of the tail. The white lateral vitta on the head is rendered more conspicuous by a short inferior streak of black along the labials, and by the lower symphysial plate being black against the white of the adjacent plates.

				millim.
Total length				137
Distance from tip of snout to ear-opening..				16
„	„	„	eye........	6
„	„	„	fore limb ..	29
„	„	„	vent	70
Length of fore limb				25
„	fourth front toe............			6
„	hind limb................			36
„	fourth hind toe.............			10
„	third hind toe			8

Characters which render this species at once conspicuous are the peculiar white markings and the toothed undersurface of the toes. The latter feature seems sufficient at once to distinguish the present

form from all the allied ones with which I have the means of comparing it. As in all other respects it is a *Cercosaura*, and would, on
account of its narrow elongate keeled dorsal scales, belong to the
subgenus *Pantodactylus*, from which it must be separated in consequence of this peculiarity of the feet, I have formed a new subgenus
Prionodactylus for its reception.

Three rather large specimens from Canelos, and one from Pallatanga.

6. LEPOSOMA[1] CARINICAUDATUM.

Lepidosoma carinicaudatum, Cope, J. Ac. Phil. viii. 1876, p. 160.

Two good-sized specimens of this very striking species from Pallatanga and two from Canelos.

7. LEPOSOMA BUCKLEYI, sp. n. (Plate XXII. fig. 2.)

Rostral plate and symphysial plate of lower jaw broad, especially the
latter. A single internasal one third broader than long ; two transverse fronto-nasals with their points in contact ; frontal moderate-
sized, triangular in front, truncated behind, longer than broad ; two
fronto-parietals ; the interparietal and two parietals are three longish
straight plates, nearly equal and uniform, evenly truncated behind
at the limit of the occipital region, and without any intervening
occipital plates. These three plates have their edges raised, forming
longitudinal ridges on the hinder portion of the head ; and the
tendency to rugosity extends also to the fronto-parietals. Four
supraorbitals. Two narrow oblique frenals. Five supralabials ; one,
extremely long, beneath the anterior part of the eye. Four infralabials. A single mental, followed by three pairs of large plates,
those of the first two pairs in contact, the third being separated by
smaller irregular-shaped plates, which go semicircularly round towards the angle of the mouth.

Temporal scales convex. Ear-opening large, rounded in front,
truncate behind. Sides of neck to shoulder also covered with round
convex scales. The whole upper surface from the parietal plates,
and the sides of the body between the fore and hind limbs as far as
the abdomen, covered with elongate lanceolate keeled scales, the
points projecting. From the regular plates of the postmental region, uniform triangular pointed scales cover the whole of the space
as far as the chest, where they form a very indistinct collar not continued into any transverse fold on the side of the neck. Scales on
the chest and anterior part of ventral surface also pointed like those
of the throat ; middle and posterior abdominal scales square, in eight
longitudinal series. Two small anterior and two large posterior
præanal scutes, some smaller ones at the sides. Upper surface of
limbs with keeled scales. Toes of fore limb very short, the inner
one minute, the third a little shorter than the fourth. Tail with
strongly keeled scales above, like the back, the keels showing a

---

[1] See Prof. Peters's recent rehabilitation of the old Spixian form of this
name, 'M.B. Ak. Berl.' 1880, p. 217.

tendency to form ridges; those on the lower surface of the tail are
also keeled.   Femoral pores fourteen.

		millim.
Total length		115
Distance from tip of snout to ear-opening		12
„ „ „ fore limb		21
„ „ „ vent		50
Length of fore limb		15
„ fourth front toe		4
„ hind limb		23
„ third hind toe		6
„ fourth hind toe		7

Upper surface pale brown, with a longitudinal row of black spots
in middle of back. A light lateral stripe from the supraorbital angle,
along the parietal border and extreme edge of the dorsal surface, to
the tail.   Sides of body black, variegated with blue or yellowish
spots on the neck.   Entire mental region yellowish, without spots.
A dark coloration predominates over the whole inferior surface of
the throat (beginning from the last postmentals), of the body, limbs,
and tail.   The scales are blackish at their root or for half their
length, and yellowish at the tips.

A single specimen from Cauelos.

This is a third species of the genus *Leposoma*, bearing a resemblance to *L. carinicaudatum*, Cope, in the pointed and carinate scales,
and also in the large præanal scutes, in which both species differ
from the *L. scincoides*, Spix, as figured by Peters in 'Abh. Ak. Berl.'
1862 (1863), pl. 2. fig. 1.   It has very much smaller scales, however, than the former species, in all the specimens of which I count
only nineteen round the body, while in the present there are not
less than thirty-four.   This great difference is made by the scales
on the sides being much smaller in the species under consideration,
while in *L. carinicaudatum* they are uniform with those of the back.
L. dispar, recently described by Prof. Peters, is evidently quite different, being more nearly allied to *L. scincoides*.

Loxopholis rugiceps, Cope, must be a Lizard very similar to both
of these species; and I am unable to see how its scutellation differs
generically from that of *Leposoma* as represented by *L. carinicaudatum*, in which Professor Cope describes " four abdominal rows of
scales with the keels reduced to an angle and mucro," consequently
smooth.   The abdominal scales are quadrate in the species which
I have now described; and this character appears to be the only one
that was left to the genus *Loxopholis* when Prof. Cope described
Leposoma carinicaudatum.

Having carefully compared the Lizard brought by Mr. Buckley
from Ecuador with the description of *Loxopholis rugiceps*, I find
that the internasal plate is much longer in that species, the præfrontals more extensively in contact, and the scales much larger,
being intermediate between those of *L. carinicaudatum* and the present
species (twenty-four round the middle of the body).   Moreover the

keels of the tail are stronger below than above, and the coloration
is quite different.

8. ECPLEOPUS (EUSPONDYLUS) GUENTHERI, sp. n.   (Plate
XXIII. fig. 1).

Form slender and elongate. Head rather narrow, not constricted
at the nape, muzzle rather long. Internasal plate large, longer than
broad, rounded in front, followed by two large, irregular, four-sided
fronto-nasals extensively in contact on their inner or smaller side;
frontal, two fronto-parietals, and large moderately broad and long
interparietal, two wedge-shaped parietals; two occipitals behind the
interparietal, smaller outer occipitals and paroccipitals above the
temporal region, the shields of which are polygonal and large.
Nasal large, triangular, with the nostril in the middle; frenal also
large, obliquely cut off posteriorly by the first and largest of a series
of rather large infraoculars. Supraorbitals four. Supralabials six,
not elongate; infralabials five, the first unusually smaller and wedge-
shaped. Symphysial very large; single mental followed by two pairs
of large contiguous postmentals; a third with their points almost
meeting, and a wide concavity behind occupied by the gular scales,
of which there are three rows before the minute gular collaret, and
seven between this and the last gular series of eight narrow and long
shields which form the collar. All these series are continuous with
those of the nape, forming complete rings of smooth quadrangular
plates, there being no granular space on the neck, and only a limited
space covered with small or minute, but not granular, scales at the
shoulder and fore part of the side. Back with cross rows of elongate
quadrangular smooth shields, about fourteen or fifteen in each row.
Small or minute lateral shields of the same type run up between the
dorsal rows. Thirty-four transverse dorsal rows from the occiput to
the root of the tail. Ventral shields elongate, quadrangular, smooth,
in ten longitudinal series (counting the smallest external ones in the
middle of the body), in twenty-one transverse rows from the collar to
the anal region. Preanal plates two large anterior, five long posterior
ones. Tail with the dorsal and ventral scutellation. Limbs covered
almost entirely with large smooth plates, leaving only a very limited
space occupied by small scales on the posterior surfaces. Femoral
pores eight. Fore limb reaching to front of eye; third and fourth
toes equal. Hind limb reaching three fourths of the length of the
side; fourth toe the longest. The inner toes are well developed on
both fore and hind feet.

Ground-colour of the entire dorsal surface uniform pale brown,
with dark bars and spots disposed as follows :—Each of the shields
on the upper surface of the head has one or more round blackish
spots; eight broad transverse bars on the back between head and
root of tail; the bars are continued at equal intervals on the tail,
diminishing to mere spots towards the end. Lower surface of body
and tail yellowish, also with round blackish spots, generally one on
each plate on the anterior portions (the gular and labial regions in
particular) being large, variegated with the dark colour, distinct bars

descending from the eye across the labials to the chin.   Limbs also spotted.   No lateral or longitudinal stripes.

		millim.
Total length	....	194
Distance from tip of snout to ear-opening..		20
„ „ „ fore limb....		37
„ „ „ vent........		92
Length of fore limb	....	27
„ fourth toe	....	9
„ hind limb	....	40
„ fourth hind toe	....	14
„ third hind toe	....	11

A single fine specimen from Sarayacu.

This fine and conspicuous species is related to *Ecpleopus* (*Euspondylus*) *maculatus*, Tschudi ; and as regards the principal characters of the head-shields, and gular and anal scutellation of that species figured by Prof. Peters, does not exhibit any marked differences.   Tschudi's figure of the entire Lizard indicates, however, a very different general appearance, more like that of *Proctoporus fraseri*, O'S., based by me on a specimen formerly confounded with *E. maculatus* in the British Museum, but differing from it in the absence of fronto-nasals.   The present species of *Euspondylus* presents a remarkable likeness to the *Gerrhonoti* named *Elgaria* by some authors.   Amongst other points of difference apparent from a comparison with the descriptions of *Euspondylus maculatus* of Tschudi and Peters, it would appear that the very well developed series of infraoculars is not distinct in Tschudi's species as figured by Peters, also that the scales are smaller, and that a longitudinal black stripe on the side of the neck is very characteristic of *Euspondylus maculatus*, while there is no such stripe in the Lizard before us, nor indeed any markings distributed longitudinally.   Moreover the black dorsal bars are very different from the quadrangular black spots described by Tschudi, and distinguish it at once from all other Lizards of this group.

9. ECPLEOPUS (EUSPONDYLUS) STRANGULATUS, Cope.

Ecpleopus (*Euspondylus*) *strangulatus*, Cope, P. Ac. Phil. 1868, p. 99.

This curious species, so different from all its congeners, is well represented in Mr. Buckley's collection, there being numerous specimens from Cauelos, two from Pallatanga, and one from Sarayacu.

SCINCIDÆ.

10. MABUIA ÆNEA (Gray).

Tiliqua ænea, Gray in Griff. An. King. ix. (Synopsis) p. 70 ; Ann. N. H. ser. 1, ii. p. 292.
Mabouya cepedii, id. Cat. Lizards in B.M. p. 95.
Eumeces mabouia, Dum. & Bibr. Erp. Gén. v. p. 646.

Copeoglossum cinctum, Tschudi, Fauna Peruana, Herpetol. p. 45, pl. 3. fig. 2.

Mabouia unimarginata, Cope, Proc. Ac. Phil. 1862, p. 187.

Two from Pallatanga, one from Sarayacu, and two from Canelos.

Professor Peters fixed the synonymy of Tschudi's Lizard in 1871, M.B. Ak. Berl. 1871, p. 400.   It is easily recognizable from the figure in the ' Fauna Peruana.'   Prof. Peters then suggested its probable identity with *Mabouya cepedii*, Gray.   I may as well take this opportunity to remark that there is in fact no difference between the single specimen so named in Gray's Catalogue and *M. ænea* (the name for this common species which apparently has the priority).

GECKOTIDÆ.

11. THECADACTYLUS RAPICAUDA (Houltuyn).

Thecadactylus rapicaudus, Gray, Cat. Liz. B.M. p. 146.

Two specimens from Canelos.

12. GONIODACTYLUS CONCINNATUS, sp. n.   (Plate XXIII. fig. 2.)

Granulation very fine all over the upper and lateral regions of the head and body, and on the gular surface, larger only on the muzzle and on a small anterior space immediately behind the mental plate, where the granules give place to rounded or polygonal scales.   Labial plates large and few in number, four upper and lower, the fourth being very small in each case.   Mental shield large; no postmental, two of the rounded anterior gular scales a little larger than the others behind it.   Scales of the entire lower surface of the body rather large, oval or rounded, beginning on the throat between the chest and the ear-opening.   Tail with broad transverse plates beneath.   Head and fore part of body above and below as far as the shoulder, and including the fore limb, pale brown or yellowish, abruptly terminated by two vertical humeral bands, sometimes meeting above and forming a regular collar of pure white with black borders.   The rest of the body, with the hind limb, blue, with black vermiculations elaborately interwoven; tail darker, with the variegations continued.   Inferior surface from chest blue, paler again at the hind limb and anal region.

				millim.
Total length				80
Distance of end of snout from ear-opening				10
,,	,,	,,	fore limb ..	20
,,	,,	,,	vent	45
Length of fore limb				18
,,	fourth front toe			5½
,,	third front toe			5
,,	hind limb			24
,,	fourth hind toe			7
,,	third hind toe			6

Three specimens from Canelos.

This Goniodactyle is very conspicuous from its coloration. The variegation of the back is something like that seen on the head only in *Goniodactylus ocellatus*, Gray, from Tobago, which seems to have remained unnoticed since the acquisition of the single type in the British Museum. The present species, from Ecuador, is quite different from that described by Dr. Günther as *Gymnodactylus caudiscutatus*, P. Z. S. 1859, p. 410, which has a round ocellus at the shoulder, but no vertical stripe.

13. GONIODACTYLUS BUCKLEYI, sp. n.   (Plate XXIII. fig. 3.)

The granulation resembling that of the preceding; the scales of the belly also similar. Mental large, and with two rounded gular scales behind, but no distinct postmental. Six supralabials, five infralabials. Tail with broad inferior scutes.

Ground-colour greyish brown. Head variegated with black; back with two parallel longitudinal rows of black blotches, pointed in front, and separated by the median line. A narrow white vertical streak on the shoulder. Gular region, from the chin to the chest, with alternating black and white oblique stripes converging behind, and making a triangular pattern.

	millim.
Total length	83
Distance from end of snout to ear-opening	11
„ „ „ fore limb ..	20
„ „ „ vent	47
Length of fore limb	18
„ third front toe	4
„ fourth front toe.............	5
„ hind limb	21
„ third hind toe	5
„ fourth hind toe.............	6

One specimen from Pallatanga and two from Canelos.
This species offers most similarity to *G. fuscus*, but does not possess the large postmental plate to which attention has been drawn by M. Bocourt.

IGUANIDÆ.

14. ENYALIUS LATICEPS.

Enyalius laticeps, Guich. Casteln. Voy. Amér. du Sud, Rept. p. 20, pl. 5 a, b; Dum. Arch. Mus. viii. p. 529.
E. planiceps, Guich. op. cit. p. 21, pl. 6, a, b.

A single specimen, 13½ inches in length, from Pallatanga.
This is the first example of the above species received by the British Museum, as those referred to it by Dr. Günther in 1859 do not really belong to it.

15. ENYALIUS MICROLEPIS, sp. n.   (Plate XXIV. fig. 2.)

Head broad, rounded, its width just before the ear-opening being nearly equal to its length from the tip of the snout to the occiput;

covered above with small convex and pointed scales closely set : larger scales forming the inner supraorbital border, and a strongly projecting superciliary border of square uniform and equal scales continuous with the canthus rostralis, about 13 from the nostril above the orbit, or from 18 to 21 in the entire series. Three large conical scales behind these at the hinder angle of the orbit ; groups of large conical scales above the temporal region, round the anterior edge of the ear, and in an isolated patch on the side of the neck. Labial shields 12, equal. A crescentic row of about twelve infra-oculars. Scales of the back and sides of the body very small. A median dorsal crest of large conical scales, beginning behind the occiput, and diminishing on the anterior part of the tail ; the highest of these scales are much less than the vertical diameter of the ear. A single lateral series of similar but much smaller scales along each side of the body from the shoulder to the fore part of the tail ; below this the scales of the side are minute and granular ; above it the dorsal scales are minute but in regular rows up to the dorsal crest, pointed and distinctly keeled ; scales of sides of gular region strongly keeled ; gular region as far as the chest with very convex erect scales closely set ; scales of the entire ventral surface, including the chest, strongly keeled, those of the limbs also keeled. Tail compressed, with complete rings of larger scales alternating with spaces in which the scales are very small ; a double series of projecting scales above ; all the scales on the inferior surface large and keeled. A single femoral pore on each side. Mottled and variegated with dark brown on a yellowish ground ; brown-tinged on the tail, or greenish, with a brown network on the sides. Gular region blackish or dark blue (in the male). Entire ventral surface yellowish. An isolated yellow spot on each side of the neck. In young specimens a yellow lateral stripe on the neck.

	millim.
Total length	160
Distance from tip of snout to ear-opening..	30
„ „ „ fore limb....	55
„ „ „ vent........	113
Length of fore limb	60
„ third finger	15
„ fourth finger................	16
„ hind limb	86
„ third toe	16
„ fourth toe...................	24

Two specimens from Sarayacu.

Besides these, there were already in the British Museum three specimens collected by Mr. Fraser in Western Ecuador, which Dr. Günther mentioned as *E. laticeps*, P. Z. S. 1859, p. 407.

The species now described approaches *E. heterolepis*, Bocourt (Ann. Sc. Nat. [5] xix. Art. No. 4, and Miss. Sc. Mex. iii. livr. 4, pl. 20 c. fig. 14), but differs from it in the much smaller size of the scales and in the single lateral series of large scales. M. Bocourt's description particularizes "deux rangées longitudinales de chaque côté de la crête dorsale;" and his figure of the general scutellation of the sides indicates about 29 scales vertically between the belly and the dorsal crest, and larger scales intermixed with these everywhere.

Sexual characters are well shown in the series of specimens before me.

The male has a larger head and longer hind limbs, reaching to the eye, while in the female they do not extend beyond the tympanum. A different system of coloration also prevails, the female being of darker brownish and more variegated tints and without the dark gular patch.

16. ENYALIUS PRÆSTABILIS, sp. n.   (Plate XXV. fig. 1.)

Head broad, with rounded and projecting lateral border of about 20 canthal and superciliary scales in a continuous series, almost uniform in shape and size. Entire upper surface of the head covered with very convex or pointed and erect scales, larger in the crescentic series bordering the supraorbital region ; larger conical scales above the temporal region. Supralabials 10, infralabials 9, uniform. Gular scales convex, elongate, the central erect. The back and sides of the body are covered with small almost uniform pointed and keeled scales, from 34 to 40 in a vertical series between the abdominal scales and the dorsal crest. Only a single very indistinct lateral series of larger scales on each side. A longitudinal crest of conical erect scales from the nape, along the median line of the back, and continued anteriorly on the tail, where it gives place to a double row or keel of pointed scales. Scales of the ventral surface small, uniform, smooth on the chest, and very feebly keeled on the middle of the abdomen ; of the limbs small and keeled. A single femoral pore in a large scale on each side. Tail compressed, ringed with small keeled scales on the sides and larger beneath.

Female with a shorter head than the male, and considerably larger scales on the sides of the body. The male also has the tail much thicker at its root and longer hind limbs, reaching to the eye, while those of the female reach only to the anterior border of the ear-opening.

Ground-colour of the upper regions of the body, in the male, reddish, very finely speckled with green ; posterior gular region and gular fold black ; lower surfaces yellowish. The female has the ground-colour above dark brown, thickly dotted over with green; tail brown- and yellow-ringed ; lower surfaces yellowish, without gular patch. A yellow spot on a patch of conical scales behind the ear in both sexes.

				millim.
Total length (of male)			....	318
Distance between end of snout and ear-opening..				34
,,	,,	,,	fore limb ..	56
,,	,,	,,	vent	126

		millim.
Length of fore limb	....	161
,,	third finger	17
,,	fourth finger	18½
,,	hind limb	197
,,	third toe	17
,,	fourth toe	27

This very handsome species differs from *E. heterolepis* in having the scales on the sides of the body much smaller and scarcely intermixed with larger ones, also in the smooth or very feebly keeled scales of the lower surface, in which, amongst other points, it differs also from *E. microlepis.*

Two specimens, male and female, nearly equal in size, from the localities Pallatanga and Canelos.

17. ANOLIS (DRACONURA) CHRYSOLEPIS.

Anolis (Draconura) chrysolepis, Dum. & Bibr. Erp. Gén. iv. p. 94; Guichenot, Castelu. Voy. Amér. Mérid. ii. p. 15, pl. iv. f. 1; Bocourt, Miss. Sc. Mex. iii. p. 99, pl. 16. f. 26.

Anolis nummifer, O'S. Ann. N. H. ser. 4, xv. p. 278.

Two specimens from Canelos, and one from Pallatanga, which show the characteristic coloration figured by Guichenot.

It is as well to state with regard to this species that the single specimen referred to it by Dr. Gray in his Catalogue is a *Norops auratus,* and that it is consequently only rather recently that we have in the British Museum possessed specimens correctly (as I believe) referred to this species.

In regard to the species which I have described as *Anolis nummifer* (Ann. N. H. ser. 4, xv. p. 278), I now entertain considerable doubts whether it is more than a variety of this same long-established *A. chrysolepis,* two distinct systems of coloration in which have been pointed out by M. Bocourt. Putting the entire series of specimens together, I now find great variation of colour, but no substantial differences but what are either sexual or within the possible limits of a species. They all have the narrower toes characteristic of *Draconura.* Another specimen, a female, which I now therefore refer to *A. chrysolepis,* was collected by Mr. Buckley at Canelos.

N.B. I may state, with reference to Prof. Cope's remarks on my identification of his *A. vittigerus* with *A. biporcatus,* that a renewed examination on the present occasion of the specimens named by him in the British Museum only confirms me in my view, and that M. Boulenger, to whom I have shown them, also agrees with me.

A variety, which must be the *A. bivittatus,* Hallow., with lateral longitudinal stripes, is well represented in this series.

[ANOLIS PUNCTATUS.

Anolis punctatus, Daudin, Rept. iv. p. 84, pl. 66. fig. 2: Dum. & Bibr. Erp. Génér. iv. p. 112.

Anolis gracilis, Neuw. Abbild. zur Nat. Brasil. pl. vii. f. 2,
Reise, ii. p. 131.

Rhinosaurus gracilis, Gray, Cat. Brit. Mus. p. 199.

Anolis nasicus, Dum. et Bibr. Erp. Génér. p. 115.

The British Museum possesses a single specimen of *A. punctatus*
from Rio Janeiro, which shows the slight differences from *A. nasicus*
indicated in the descriptions of Duméril and Bibron. Of this latter
species there are also four examples, all males, while the other is a
female. I cannot resist the conclusion indicated in the above revised
synonymy, in which, of course, the older name of Daudin takes
precedence.]

The fine specimen in Mr. Buckley's collection which I formerly
named *A. nasicus* (P. Z. S. 1880, p. 491) does not really belong to
that species, only superficially resembling it, and is apparently an
undescribed one, which I have pleasure in naming after my friend
M. Boulenger:—

18. ANOLIS BOULENGERI, sp. n.   (Plate XXIV. fig. 1.)

Head elongate; muzzle raised; præfrontal space concave; anterior
upper portions of head covered with rounded or polygonal scales,
moderate-sized, slightly convex on the muzzle, flat on the frontal
region. Orbital semicircles of very large scales, separated on the
vertex by the interorbitals, which have dwindled to one or two very
small scales in a single series. A central group of large supraorbitals surrounded by small rounded or polygonal ones. A single
long anterior supraocular continuous with the long canthal scales.
Occipital plate large, rounded, very little longer than wide, larger
than the ear-opening. Six series of frenals. Seven supralabials;
eight infralabials, with large scales in several rows beneath. Scales
of the entire upper surface and sides uniform, minute, granular;
those of the ventral surface very small, rounded, and distinctly
carinate. Toes with broad dilatations. Tail long.

Bright green, with round pearl-like white spots in transverse rows
on the back and sides. Lower parts yellowish.

			millim.
Total length			280
Length of snout to the eye			11
Distance from tip of snout to ear-opening			21
,,	,,	,, fore limb	35
,,	,,	,, vent	79
Length of fore limb			32
,,	third and fourth front toes		8
,,	hind limb		57
,,	third hind toe		9¼
,,	fourth hind toe		14

From Canelos. This species shows a remarkable analogy to *A.
punctatus* in the shape of the head, proportions of the body and
coloration, the white spots being very similar. It is, distinguished,
however, by the keeled ventral scales, those of *A. punctatus* being
flat and smooth. A peculiarity which I have remarked in all the

specimens, both male and female, of the latter species, is a median longitudinal groove on the belly from behind the præanal region, the scales bordering the groove on each side being enlarged.

19. ANOLIS FUSCO-AURATUS.

Anolis fusco-auratus, D'Orbigny, Voy. Amér. Mérid. Rept. pl. 3. fig. 2; Dum. & Bibr. Erp. Gén. iv. p. 110; Bocourt, Nouv. Arch. Mus. 1869, vi. Bullet. p. 15; id. Miss. Sc. Mex. iii. pl. 14. figs. 16, 16 a.

Anolis viridiænens, Peters, M.B. Ak. Berl. 1863, p. 147.

One specimen, a female, from Pallatanga.

20. ANOLIS BUCKLEYI.

Anolis buckleyi, O'Shaughnessy, P. Z. S. 1880, p. 492, pl. 49.

The two specimens of this beautiful species obtained by Mr. Buckley have already been described.

21. ANOLIS BOUVIERI.

Anolis bouvieri, Bocourt, Miss. Sc. Mex. iii. p. 58, pl. 14. fig. 8.

Two specimens, apparently of this species, from Pallatanga and Canelos. M. Bocourt's type was from Guatemala. Specimens already identified by me in the British Museum as *A. bouvieri* are from Pebas and from Guayaquil. The one from the latter locality is that enumerated by Dr. Günther as *A. æneus* in his list of Mr. Fraser's collection (P. Z. S. 1859, p. 89). *Anolis æneus*, Gray, however, cannot be looked upon as a species, since the single specimen on which it appears to have been founded proves to be only a young *Anolis alligator*, D. & B. See O'Shaughnessy, Ann. N. H. ser. 4, vol. xv. p. 272.

22. LEIOCEPHALUS ACULEATUS.

Leiocepalus aculeatus, O'Shaughnessy, Ann. N. H. ser. 5, vol. iv. p. 303 (1879).

Four additional specimens from Canelos and Pallatanga afford me the opportunity of giving some further particulars about this remarkable species. On each side of the occiput are some erect scales, forming a flag-like border. These curious scales, which are not conical, are present in both sexes, and appear characteristic of the species, as they are not seen in *L. iridescens* nor, of course, in the species of the genus with small cephalic shields.

The sexes are very distinct. The male is of much darker coloration, as previously described, and has the whole gular region deep black. It has also the tail covered with very large scales, and very strongly compressed, almost resembling *Basiliscus* in this respect. The female has the back light brown, with triangular bars of darker pointing backwards. The sides below the lateral crest are dark brown, sharply separated from the lighter hue of the back. The tail is compressed at the root only, rounded afterwards. This species would belong to the same section of *Leiocephalus* as *L. hermi-nieri*, D. & B., which also has the ventral scales keeled. That species is unrepresented in the British Museum, as Bibron's supposition of its identity with *L. carinatus* appears to have been incorrect, although very confidently expressed. The description indicates, however, a cephalic scutellation totally different from the present species, a very much higher crest, and other conspicuous points of difference. The scales on the top of the muzzle in the present species are quite large, only about 10 in number, and not keeled, instead of the 30 very small keeled ones mentioned by Bibron.

23. LEIOCEPHALUS TRACHYCEPHALUS.

Leiocephalus trachycephalus, Dum. Cat. Méth. Rept.1851, p. 70; Arch. Mus. viii. p. 539, pl. 23. fig. 1.

One specimen from Sarayacu, Ecuador. There are now numerous specimens in the British Museum which I have recognized as of this species; the figure of the entire lizard, however, evidently a very bad one, shows little resemblance to them.

24. HOPLOCERCUS ANNULARIS, sp. n. (Plate XXV. fig. 2.)

Scales on snout convex, granular, similar and nearly uniform on the other parts of the head, excepting the supraorbital spaces, where they are larger and rounded or polygonal. The upper surface of the body is covered with a groundwork of small granular scales, with tubercles in several complete longitudinal rows from the nape to the root of the tail, more closely set along the median line of the back; series of tubercles also descend vertically on the sides. Scales of the belly rather small, but regularly tessellated. Supralabials nine. Infralabials ten. Limbs strongly tubercular. Tail longer than head and body, cylindrical, and surrounded at regular and rather close intervals throughout its entire length by complete rings of projecting tubercles or spinous scales. A series of two or three very large femoral pores on each thigh. Teeth trilobate.

Brown, with transverse dark bars on the back. An oblique yellow black-bordered stripe in front of the fore limb. A large yellow spot on the upperside of the thigh.

	millim.
Total length	132
Length of head to ear-opening	16
Distance from tip of snout to fore limb	27
,, ,, ,, vent	59
Length of fore limb	24
,, third and fourth fingers	8
,, hind limb	40
,, fourth toe	14

A single specimen, evidently young, as shown by an external groove indicating imperfect symphysis of the lower jaw, was obtained from Canelos. It is a very interesting form, which, on account of the total dissimilarity of its tail, might have been separated generically from *Hoplocercus spinosus*. I can, however, detect no other grounds for such separation; and as I have lately found a

precisely analogous case in the Agamidæ, in which I felt loth to
create an artificial genus, I have acted in the same way in the present instance. The *Uromastix princeps* recently described by me
(P. Z. S. 1880, p. 445) has an abnormally flattened spinous tail of
extraordinary appearance, but somewhat like the tail of *H. spinosus*.
It consequently differs from the other species of *Uromastix* with
long verticillated tails, in just the same way as *H. spinosus* differs
from the present species. In other respects these two species are
so similar that it is difficult to draw up a complete specific diagnosis
of the new one. There are, however, fewer labial shields; and the
limbs are considerably longer, the hind ones reaching to the front of
the ear, while in *H. spinosus* they reach only to the shoulder.

25. PLICA UMBRA, Gray.

One young specimen from Pallatanga.

26. URANOCENTRUM FLAVICEPS, Guichenot.

One adult and two young from Canelos, and one adult from
Sarayacu in Ecuador. There is a locality of the same name
(Sarayacu) in Peru.

27. URANISCODON UMBRA, Kaup.

A single specimen from Sarayacu, Ecuador.

EXPLANATION OF THE PLATES.

PLATE XXII.

Fig. 1. *Cercosaura (Pantodactylus) reticulata*, p. 230.
  1 *a*. —— (——) ——, head above.
  1 *b*. —— (——) ——, dorsal scutes.
  1 *c*. —— (——) ——, ventral scutes.
  2. *Leposoma buckleyi*, p. 233.
  2 *a*. —— ——, half undersurface.
  2 *b*. —— ——, scales of back.
  3. *Cercosaura (Prionodactylus) manicata*, p. 231.
  3 *a*. —— (——) ——, under surface of fingers.

PLATE XXIII.

Fig. 1. *Ecpleopus (Euspondylus) guentheri*, entire, p. 235.
  2. *Gonodactylus concinnatus*, p. 237, entire.
  3. —— *buckleyi*, p. 238, entire.

PLATE XXIV.

Fig. 1. *Anolis boulengeri*, p. 242.
  1 *a*. —— ——, head from above.
  2. *Enyalius microlepis*, p. 238.

PLATE XXV.

Fig. 1. *Enyalius præstabilis*, p. 240.
  1 *a*. —— ——, scutellation of side.
  2. *Hoplocercus annularis*, p. 244.

5. Description of a new Species of *Enyalius* in the Brussels
Museum. By G. A. BOULENGER.

[Received January 19, 1881.]

(Plate XXVI.)

In a paper on the collection of Reptiles made in Ecuador, and
presented to the Brussels Museum by Consul Emile de Ville, I have
mentioned[1] a specimen of *Enyalius*, which I identified with *E.
heterolepis*, Bocourt, noticing, however, that the dorsal crest was
more elevated in my specimen than in the typical one. Having
reexamined the former, and compared it with examples of the two
beautiful species just described by Mr. O'Shaughnessy, viz. *E. microlepis* and *E. præstabilis*, I am now convinced that it belongs to a
distinct, hitherto undescribed species, which I have the pleasure of
naming

ENYALIUS OSHAUGHNESSYI, sp. n.   (Plate XXVI.)

Head broad and rounded, once and two thirds as long as broad,
covered with subquadrangular strongly keeled scales, those on the
canthus rostralis and the superciliary border a good deal larger and
projecting. A small but distinct occipital plate. Loreal region
concave, with small, irregular, keeled scales. Temporal region with
small convex scales, above with a series of large conical ones; a few
large conical scales near the tympanum. Labial shields 14, equal.
Scales of the back and sides of the body small, smooth and slightly
keeled, irregularly intermixed with larger but not conical ones. A
median dorsal crest of very large conical scales, beginning behind
the occiput, and gradually diminishing in height to the base of the
tail, where it becomes double and soon vanishes; the highest of
these scales on the neck measure more than the vertical diameter
of the ear-opening. A single lateral series of conical scales on each
side of the back, beginning at a small distance behind the ear, and
extending to the sacral region. There are about 12 longitudinal
rows of scales between the dorsal crest and the lateral series, and 30
between the latter and the belly. Scales on the limbs strongly
keeled. Scales of gular region keeled; those of the pectoral and
ventral regions as large as those upon the limbs, and strongly
keeled. A single femoral pore on each side. Tail compressed,
with verticillate, strongly keeled scales, the verticilli composed of
five or six rings of increasing size; scales of the lower surface equal
and also strongly keeled.

Coloration (in the single male specimen). General colour dark
brown; throat and some of the scales of the sides of the body
and tail and some of the limbs greenish; a light rounded spot on
each side of the neck, behind the ear: gular fold black.

[1] Bull. Soc. Zool. France, 1880, p. 43.

Dimensions.   millim.

Total length (the tip of the tail is broken off) 310
From tip of snout to ear-opening 43
  ,,   ,,   ,,   fore limb 53
  ,,   ,,   ,,   vent 135
Length of fore limb 72
  ,,   ,, third finger 17
  ,,   ,, fourth finger 19
  ,,   ,, hind limb 95
  ,,   ,, third toe 19
  ,,   ,, fourth toe 28

This species is allied to *E. heterolepis, E. microlepis,* and *E. præstabilis,* but differs from all three in the higher dorsal crest, from *E. heterolepis* in the scales of the body, which are smaller (about 42 vertically in the present species, and 29 in *E. heterolepis*) and not intermixed with *conical* ones, and in the absence of a second lateral series of large scales; from *E. microlepis* in the larger, slightly or not keeled dorsal scales; from *E. præstabilis* in the shape of the dorsal scales, and especially in the strongly keeled pectoral and ventral ones.

EXPLANATION OF PLATE XXVI.

Fig. 1. *Enyalius oshaughnessyi.* 1 *a,* scutellation of the side of ditto.
Fig. 2. Scutellation of the side of *E. microlepis.*

6. Remarks upon the Habits of the Darter (*Plotus anhinga*). By A. D. BARTLETT, Superintendent of the Society's Gardens.

[Received Jan. 6, 1881.]

At a meeting of this Society in 1869 (see P.Z.S. 1869, p. 142) I read a paper upon the habits of the Hornbills, and called attention to the fact that, from time to time, these birds cast up a substance that is found upon examination to be the epithelial lining of the gizzard. I now bring before the Society a notice of another instance of this remarkable habit, in a very different group of birds. A Darter (*Plotus anhinga*), the bird I now speak of, was received on the 18th of July 1880, and since that time has appeared to be in *perfect health,* and has fed regularly. It has thrown up the lining of its stomach on three or four occasions during this period; but unfortunately the keeper, not being aware of the interest that would be attached to the circumstance, and not knowing the nature of the substance, carelessly threw the castings away. I happened, however, to be present when the last sac was thrown up, and secured it for examination, and have handed it over to our Prosector, Mr. Forbes, for that purpose.

This remarkable fact being now known to occur in two widely

separate genera of birds, induces me to believe, that the habit may
exist in many other birds and have hitherto been unobserved.   In
many cases the substance would sink to the bottom of the water,
where it would soon decompose; and this may account for its not
having been previously noticed.

I feel particularly anxious to call the attention of persons keeping
Cormorants, and of those persons visiting the haunts of Cormorants,
to this habit, as it is highly probable that this bird does the same .
thing.

7. Note on Mr. Bartlett's Communication on the Habits
of the Darter. By W. A. FORBES, B.A., Prosector to
the Society.

[Received February 1, 1881.]

The specimen put into my hands by Mr. Bartlett is a somewhat
broken bag-like sac, which is undoubtedly the shed " epithelial " coat
of the gizzard of the Darter. Where the "epithelium"[1] is thickest and
best developed, at the bottom of the gizzard, the walls have remained
intact; but above, where it thins off towards the pyloric and œsophageal
openings, · they have become broken, so that the sac is widely open
here. A small patch of the characteristic hairs (cf. Garrod, P. Z. S.
1876, p. 343, pl. xxviii. fig. 2) of the pyloric part of the gizzard
has come away with the epithelium ; these alone would suffice to
indicate the bird whence it was derived. The hard epithelium does
not extend above the limits of the gizzard : hence none of the mucous
coverings of the proventricular gland or œsophagus has been preserved
in the ejected specimen. The outer surface of the cast epithelium is
smooth and velvety, and exactly similar in appearance to epithelium
that has been peeled off the muscular walls of the gizzard artificially.

A microscopical examination of a part of the cast epithelium shows
that it is quite identical in structure with that of the unshed epithelium
of the stomach.

I may add that in the stomach of a lately dead example of the
species—though not that of the individual which " moulted " its
stomach, which is still (February 1) alive and in good health—there
is some appearance of a similar " moult " being about to take place,
the epithelial layer being easily detached from the subjacent ones,
whilst beneath it there is apparently a new, though still very thin,
coat of epithelium in course of formation. This appearance is con-
firmed by sections of the epithelium.

[1] I use this term in the same sense as many previous writers have done, as a
convenient term for the object in question, without committing myself to any
opinion as to its true nature.—W. A. F.

LIST OF THE PUBLICATIONS

ZOOLOGICAL SOCIETY OF LONDON.

The scientific publications of the Zoological Society are of two kinds — "Proceedings," published in an octavo form, and "Transactions," in quarto.

According to the present arrangements, the "Proceedings" contain not only notices of all business transacted at the scientific meetings, but also all the papers read at such meetings and recommended to be published by the Committee of Publication. From fifty to seventy coloured plates and engravings are attached to each annual volume of the "Proceedings," to illustrate the new or otherwise remarkable species of animals described in them. Amongst such illustrations, figures of the new or rare species acquired in a living state for the Society's Gardens are often given.

The "Proceedings" for each year are issued in four parts, on the first of the months of June, August, October, and April, the part published in April completing the volume for the preceding year. They may be obtained with black or coloured illustrations.

The "Transactions" contain such of the more important communications made to the scientific meetings of the Society as, on account of the nature of the plates required to illustrate them, are better adapted for publication in the quarto form.

Fellows, and Honorary, Foreign, and Corresponding Members, upon payment of a Subscription of £1 1s. before the day of the Anniversary Meeting in each year, are entitled to receive all the Society's Publications for the year. They are likewise entitled to purchase the Publications of the Society at 25 per cent. less than the price charged for them to the Public. A further reduction of 25 per cent. is made upon purchases of Publications issued prior to 1861, if they exceed the value of five pounds.

The following is a complete list of the publications of the Society already issued. They may be obtained at the Society's Office (11 Hanover Square, W.), at Messrs. Longmans', the Society's publishers (Paternoster Row, E.C.), or through any bookseller :—

[June 1, 1881.]

PROCEEDINGS OF THE COMMITTEE OF SCIENCE AND CORRE-SPONDENCE OF THE ZOOLOGICAL SOCIETY OF LONDON.

8vo. 2 vols.

			To Fellows.	To the Public.
Part I.	1830–31.	1 vol. 8vo................... Price	4s. 6d. ...	6s.
„ II.	1832.	„ .... „	4s. 6d. ...	6s.

PROCEEDINGS OF THE ZOOLOGICAL SOCIETY OF LONDON.

8vo. 15 vols. and Index. (First Series.)

			Price to Fellows.	Price to the Public.					Price to Fellows.	Price to the Public.
Part	I. 1833.	1 vol. 8vo.	4s. 6d. ...	6s.	Part	IX. 1841.	1 vol. 8vo.	4s. 6d. ...	6s.
„	II. 1834.	„	4s. 6d. ...	6s.	„	X. 1842.	„	4s. 6d. ...	6s.
„	III. 1835.	„	4s. 6d. ...	6s.	„	XI. 1843.	„	4s. 6d. ...	6s.
„	IV. 1836	„	4s. 6d. ...	6s.	„	XII. 1844.	„	4s. 6d. ...	6s.
„	V. 1837.	„	4s. 6d. ...	6s.	„	XIII. 1845.	„	4s. 6d. ...	6s.
„	VI. 1838.	„	4s. 6d. ...	6s.	„	XIV. 1846.	„	4s. 6d. ...	6s.
„	VII. 1839.	„	4s. 6d. ...	6s.	„	XV. 1847.	„	4s. 6d. ...	6s.
„	VIII. 1840.	„	4s. 6d. ...	6s.	Index 1830–47.		„	4s. 6d. ...	6s.

PROCEEDINGS OF THE ZOOLOGICAL SOCIETY OF LONDON.

8vo. 13 vols. and Index. (Second Series.)

			Letterpress only.			With Plates Coloured.	
			To Fellows.	To the Public.		To Fellows. £ s. d.	To the Public. £ s. d.
Part	XVI. 1848.	1 vol. 8vo.	4s. 6d.	... 6s.	... Price	1 1 0 ...	1 7 6
„	XVII. 1849.	„	4s. 6d.	... 6s.	... „	1 1 0 ...	1 7 6
„	XVIII. 1850.	„	4s. 6d.	... 6s.	... „	1 7 6 ...	1 18 0
„	XIX. 1851.	„	4s. 6d.	... 6s.	... „	0 16 0* ...	1 1 0*
„	XX. 1852.	„	4s. 6d.	... 6s.	... „	0 16 0* ...	1 1 0*
„	XXI. 1853.	„	4s. 6d.	... 6s.	... „	0 18 0 ...	1 4 0
„	XXII. 1854.	„	4s. 6d.	... 6s.	... „	1 0 0 ...	1 6 0
„	XXIII. 1855.	„	4s. 6d.	... 6s.	... „	1 7 6* ...	1 18 0*
„	XXIV. 1856.	„	4s. 6d.	... 6s.	... „	1 1 0 ...	1 7 6
„	XXV. 1857.	„	4s. 6d.	... 6s.	... „	1 1 0 ...	1 7 6
„	XXVI. 1858.	„	4s. 6d.	... 6s.	... „	1 12 0 ...	2 2 0
„	XXVII. 1859.	„	4s. 6d.	... 6s.	... „	1 12 0* ...	2 2 0*
„	XXVIII. 1860.	„	4s. 6d.	... 6s.	... „	1 12 0 ...	2 2 0
Index 1848–60.		„	4s. 6d.	... 6s.			

ILLUSTRATIONS TO THE PROCEEDINGS OF THE ZOOLOGICAL SOCIETY OF LONDON, 1848–60. 8vo. 6 vols.

		Plates Uncoloured.			Plates Coloured.	
		To Fellows. £ s. d.	To the Public. £ s. d.		To Fellows. £ s. d.	To the Public. £ s. d.
Mammalia	1 vol.,	1 2 6 ...	1 10 0	... Price	2 8 0 ...	3 3 0
Aves	2 vols.,	2 8 0 ...	3 3 0	... „	4 15 0* ...	6 6 0*
Reptilia et Pisces ...	1 vol.,	0 15 9 ...	1 1 0	... „	1 3 0 ...	1 10 0
Mollusca...............	1 vol.,	0 15 9 ...	1 1 0	... „	1 3 0 ...	1 10 0
Annulosa et Radiata	1 vol.,	1 11 6 ...	2 2 0	... „	2 3 0* ...	3 3 0*

* No copies of these volumes remain in stock.

3

PROCEEDINGS OF THE SCIENTIFIC MEETINGS OF THE ZOOLOGICAL SOCIETY OF LONDON.

	Complete.		Letterpress only.		Illustrations only.	
	To Fellows.	To the Public.	To Fellows.	To the Public.	To Fellows.	To the Public.
1861, cloth	32s.	47s.	4s. 6d.	6s.	27s. 6d.	41s.
1862, ,,	32s.	47s.	4s. 6d.	6s.	27s. 6d.	41s.
1863, ,,	32s.	47s.	4s. 6d.	6s.	27s. 6d.	41s.
1864, ,,	32s.	47s.	4s. 6d.	6s.	27s. 6d.	41s.
1865, ,,	32s.	47s.	4s. 6d.	6s.	27s. 6d.	41s.
1866, ,,	32s.	47s.	4s. 6d.	6s.	27s. 6d.	41s.

	With Illustrations Uncoloured.		With Illustrations Coloured.	
	To Fellows.	To the Public.	To Fellows.	To the Public.
1867, cloth	11s. 6d.	14s. 6d.	32s. 6d.	47s. 6d.
1868, ,,	11s. 6d.	14s. 6d.	32s. 6d.	47s. 6d.
1869, ,,	11s. 6d.	14s. 6d.	32s. 6d.	47s. 6d.
1870, ,,	11s. 6d.	14s. 6d.	32s. 6d.	47s. 6d.
Index, 1861-1870	4s. 6d.	6s. 0d.		
1871, cloth	11s. 6d.	14s. 6d.	32s. 6d.	47s. 6d.
1872, ,,	11s. 6d.	14s. 6d.	32s. 6d.	47s. 6d.
1873, ,,	11s. 6d.	14s. 6d.	32s. 6d.	47s. 6d.
1874, ,,	11s. 6d.	14s. 6d.	38s. 6d.	50s. 6d.
1875, ,,	11s. 6d.	14s. 6d.	38s. 6d.	50s. 6d.
1876, ,,	11s. 6d.	14s. 6d.	38s. 6d.	50s. 6d.
1877, ,,	11s. 6d.	14s. 6d.	38s. 6d.	50s. 6d.
1878, ,,	11s. 6d.	14s. 6d.	38s. 6d.	50s. 6d.
1879, ,,	11s. 6d.	14s. 6d.	38s. 6d.	50s. 6d.
1880, ,,	11s. 6d.	14s. 6d.	38s. 6d.	50s. 6d.
1881, part 1 (Jan. & Feb.)	2s. 3d.	3s. 0d.	9s. 0d.	12s. 0d.

TRANSACTIONS OF THE ZOOLOGICAL SOCIETY OF LONDON. 4to. 10 vols. and Four Parts.

					To Fellows.			To the Public.		
					£	s.	d.	£	s.	d.
Vol. I.,	containing 59 Plates	(1833-35)	Price	3	13	6	...	4	18	0*
Vol. II.,	,, 71 ,,	(1835-41)	,,	4	0	0	...	5	6	6*
Vol. III.,	,, 63 ,,	(1842-49)	,,	3	8	6	...	4	11	0*
Vol. IV.,	,, 78 ,,	(1851-62)	,,	6	2	0	...	8	2	6*
Vol. V.,	,, 67 ,,	(1862-66)	,,	5	3	6	...	6	19	0
Vol. VI.,	,, 91 ,,	(1866-69)	,,	11	5	0	..	15	0	0
Vol. VII.,	,, 73 ,,	(1869-72)	,,	8	17	0	...	11	16	0
Vol. VIII.,	,, 82 ,,	(1872-74)	,,	9	8	3	...	12	11	0
Vol. IX.,	,, 99 ,,	(1875-77)	,,	12	0	0	...	16	0	0
Vol. X.,	,, 94 ,,	(1877-79)	,,	10	0	6	...	13	7	0
Vol. XI., part 1,	containing 4 plates	(Jan. 1880)	,,	0	12	0	...	0	16	0
Vol. XI., ,, 2,	,, 7 ,,	(Aug. 1880)	,,	0	18	0	...	1	4	0
Vol. XI., ,, 3,	,, 8 ,,	(Mar. 1881)	,,	1	2	6	...	1	10	0
Vol. XI., ,, 4,	,, 3 ,,	(Apr. 1881)	,,	0	7	6	...	0	10	0

* Only imperfect copies of these volumes remain in stock.

LISTS OF THE ANIMALS IN THE SOCIETY'S GARDENS.

List of Vertebrated Animals Living in the Gardens of the Zoological Society of London. 8vo. 1862. Price 1s. 6d.

List of Vertebrated Animals Living in the Gardens of the Zoological Society of London. (Second Edition.) 8vo. 1863.
Price 1s. 6d.

List of Vertebrated Animals Living in the Gardens of the Zoological Society of London. (Third Edition.) 8vo. 1865.
Price 1s. 6d.

List of Vertebrated Animals Living in the Gardens of the Zoological Society of London. (Fourth Edition.) 8vo. 1866.
Price 1s. 6d.

Revised List of the Vertebrated Animals now or lately Living in the Gardens of the Zoological Society of London. 8vo. 1872.
Price 2s.

Revised List of the Vertebrated Animals now or lately Living in the Gardens of the Zoological Society of London.—Supplement, containing Additions received in 1872, 1873, and 1874. 8vo. 1875. Price 1s.

List of the Vertebrated Animals now or lately Living in the Gardens of the Zoological Society of London. (Sixth Edition.) 8vo. 1877. Price 3s. 6d.

List of the Vertebrated Animals now or lately Living in the Gardens of the Zoological Society of London. (Seventh Edition.) 8vo. 1879. Price 3s. 6d.

List of the Vertebrated Animals now or lately Living in the Gardens of the Zoological Society of London.—First Supplement, containing Additions received in 1879. 8vo. 1880.
Price 1s. 6d.

Such of these publications as are in stock may be obtained at the Society's Office (11 Hanover Square, W.), at Messrs. Longmans', the Society's publishers (Paternoster Row, E.C.), or through any bookseller.

Price 6d., Sewed,

A GUIDE TO THE GARDENS
OF THE
ZOOLOGICAL SOCIETY OF LONDON.

Thirty-fifth Edition, corrected according to the present Arrangement of the Gardens,

BY PHILIP LUTLEY SCLATER, M.A., Ph.D., F.R.S.,
SECRETARY TO THE SOCIETY,

London: BRADBURY, AGNEW, AND Co., 10 Bouverie Street; and at the Society's Gardens in the Regent's Park.

Contents (*continued*).

LIST OF PLATES.

1881.

PART I.

NOTICE.

According to present arrangements the 'Proceedings' are issued in *four* parts, as follows:—

Part I. containing papers read in January and February, on June 1st.
,, II. ,, ,, ,, March and April, on August 1st.
,, III. ,, ,, , May and June, on October 1st.
,, IV. ,, ,, ,, November and December, on April 1st.

The price is 12s. per part for the edition with coloured, and 3s. per part for that with uncoloured Plates.

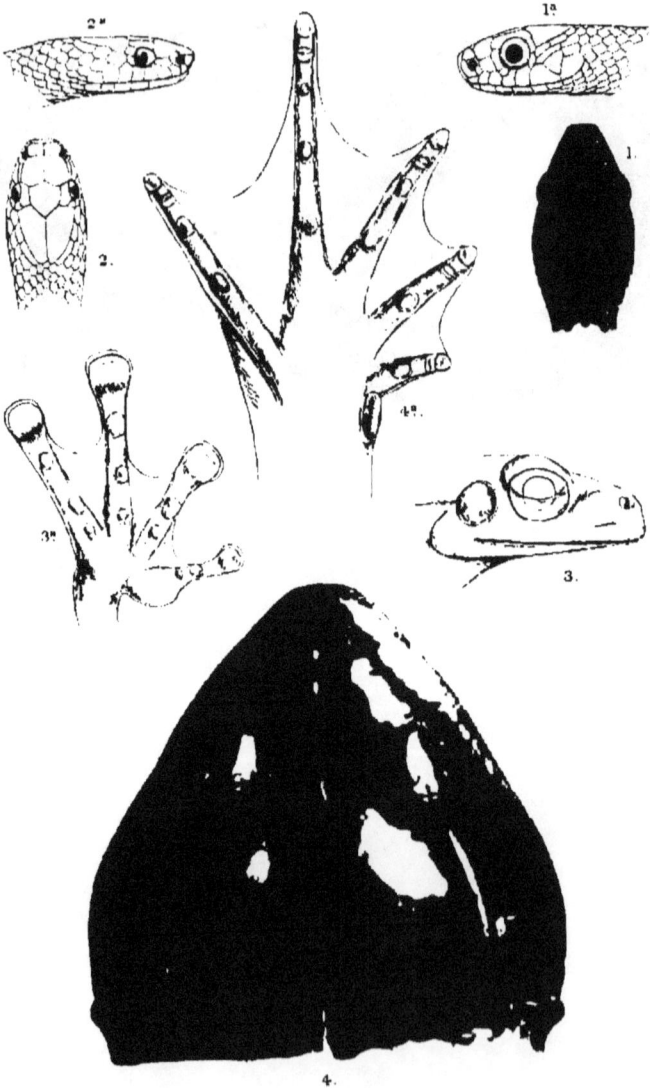

R.Mintern del et lith.   Mintern Bros imp

1 SIMOTES DENNYSI.   3. RHACOPHORUS DENNYSI.
2 OPHITES SUBCINCTUS.   4. RANA MACRODON.

PLATE XIII

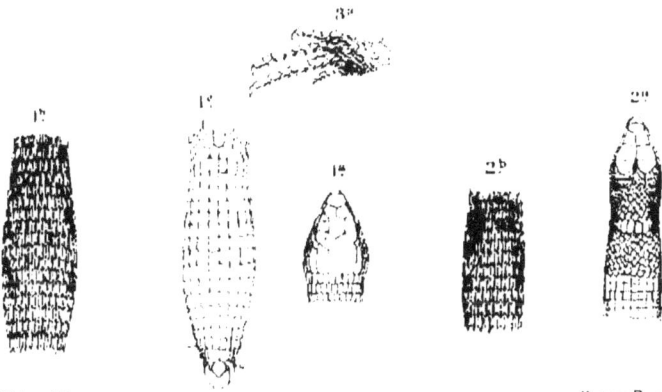

P. Mintern lith.

Mintern Bros. imp.

1. CERCOSAURA RETICULATA.
2. LEPOSOMA BUCKLEYI.
3. CERCOSAURA MANICATA.

R. Mintern Bros. lith.   Madam Pacis imp.

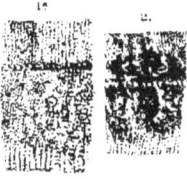

J. Mintern lith.

1. ENYALIUS O'SHAUGHNESSYI.
2. E.   "   MICROLEPIS.

Mintern Bros. imp.